GW01288254

50 THINGS TO TRY ON HOLIDAY

This book belongs to:

....

....

Age:...

I live in:.......................................

A picture of me

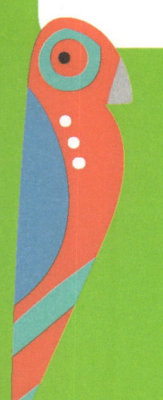

With thanks to my niece and
nephew, Amy and Joseph, who
helped write this book.
– Kim

Published by b small publishing ltd.
www.bsmall.co.uk

1 2 3 4 5   ISBN 978-1-912909-09-4

Production by Madeleine Ehm. Editorial by Sam Hutchinson.
Design by Kim Hankinson. Cover design by Vicky Barker.

Printed in China by WKT Co. Ltd.

British Library Cataloguing-in-Publication Data. A catalogue record for this book is available
from the British Library.

Activities for ...

... dancing, daring, dreaming, writing, collecting, exploring, travelling, mindful, never-bored ADVENTURERS!

KIM HANKINSON

HOW TO
USE THIS BOOK

This book is full of daring-looking-thinking-listening activities everyone can try. Starting on any page, do as many activities as you can fit into a day and in any order you like.

The activities are colour coded to help you choose what sort of activity you would like to do. Match the activity key below with the coloured circle in the contents list opposite or the coloured circle enclosing each page number throughout the book. There are extra pages for notes and doodles throughout the book.

Have fun and have a great trip!

ACTIVITY KEY

| EXPLORE  | DARE | MOVE | MAKE | RECORD | CAREFUL! |

Always ask an adult when you see a red warning symbo

Travel track

HOME

CONTENTS CHECKLIST:

Record your journey from home along the travel track. Add more paper if you need.

DAILY DARE

Try a super-chilled activity.

MEDITATE

MAKE BRACELETS

CAT-NAP

MAKE A MANDALA

To continue each piece of the mandala, draw the reflection of the section beside and colour in.

Imagine

Write a story inspired by your trip. Fill in
the notes below while you are on your
trip, and use them to get started.

Beginning

Memorable weather: ....

Where you went: ....

Holiday companion: ....

Middle

A place you had fun: ....

Someone you met: ....

Something strange that happened: ....

....

A weird animal: ....

Happy Ending

An object you noticed: ....

Something funny that happened: ....

....

Get wet!

Rainy day? Don't mope. Get outside!

UMBRELLA-DANCING

PUDDLE-SPLASHING

CATCHING RAIN IN YOUR MOUTH

SINGING IN THE RAIN

Big city sights

Soak up the city and find these sights.

FOUNTAIN

BUS

JOGGER

PARK

BIG CLOCK

MONUMENT

STREET
FOOD

TAXI

SKYSCRAPER

How many clouds can you see?

Write your name in bubble writing.

Colour palette

Look out for every
colour in the palette.

DAILY DARE

Try one of these acrobatic activities.

CARTWHEEL

HANDSTAND

CRANE

These are good to try on the grass in a park or garden, as you might need a soft landing...

Eco-bingo

How many of these natural
environments can you visit?

RIVERSIDE

DESERT

SEA

FOREST

GRASSLAND

MOUNTAIN

New skills

Try a new activity and discover new skills!

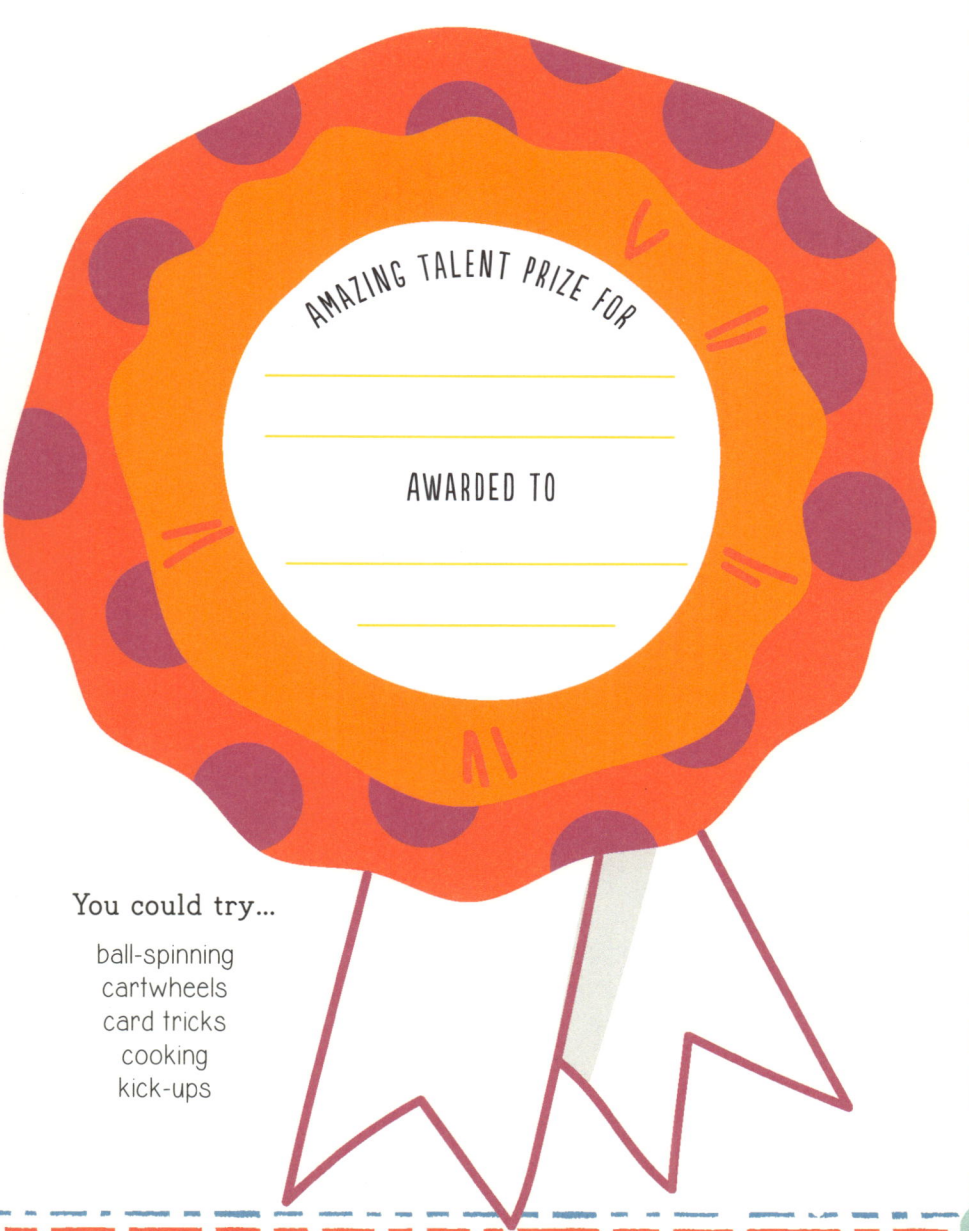

AMAZING TALENT PRIZE FOR

AWARDED TO

You could try...

ball-spinning
cartwheels
card tricks
cooking
kick-ups

Invent a new shape!

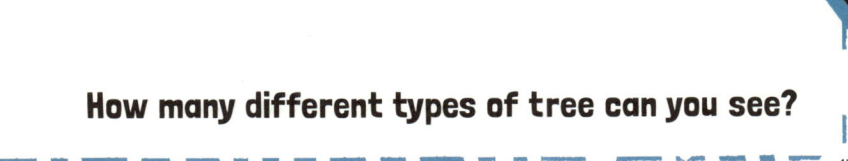

How many different types of tree can you see?

All I got was this T-shirt

Design an awesome holiday T-shirt.

Follow the leader

Every day let a different person in your group lead the way. Follow in single file and make sure everyone has a go at being in charge.

I was leader on: ....

At: ....

FUN THIS WAY

Super stars

Look into the night sky. Can you find one of the constellations that help you find North?

SOUTHERN HEMISPHERE

1. Find the Southern Cross, which is a cross-shaped cluster of stars.

SOUTHERN CROSS

2. Find the two stars known as the Pointers nearby.

THE POINTERS

SOUTH IS DIRECTLY BELOW THIS POINT --->

3. Create imaginary lines in the night sky from these two constellations as shown. Directly below where those two lines meet on the horizon is South.

NORTHERN HEMISPHERE

NORTH STAR

1. First, look for the Big Dipper. It's shaped like a big saucepan.

LITTLE DIPPER

2. Imagine a line going up from the front of the pan, just like the line shown.

3. It will lead to Polaris, or the North Star. Identify the Little Dipper to make sure you have found the right star. The North Star is the tip of its handle.

BIG DIPPER

4. You can follow Polaris anywhere in the Northern Hemisphere, and it will always take you north.

Wish you were here!

Write a postcard to a relative, friend or pet.

Use this space to practise...

_____

_____

_____

_____

_____

...or to design your own!

Bush skills

Try these wild holiday activities.

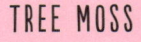

TREE MOSS

NATURE'S COMPASS

In the Northern Hemisphere, thicker tree moss and spiders' webs are mostly found on the north-facing side of trees and logs, as that is where they are sheltered from the hot, drying sunshine. In the Southern Hemisphere, the opposite is true, and you will find these things on the south-facing side.

SPIDER'S WEB

TRACKING

You can tell where an animal has been by looking for these signs.

BROKEN TWIGS

FOOTPRINTS/TRACKS

FUNNY SMELLS ...AND POOP!

NIBBLED PLANTS

MARKET FORAGING

Look out for food found growing wild. But beware, a lot of things are poisonous so do not pick or eat anything unless approved by a qualified guide.

HERB

MUSHROOM

BERRY

For a taste of local wild food, you can also hunt in a local market.

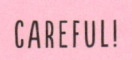

CAREFUL!

Sit still for as long as you can!

Challenge someone to a game of noughts and crosses!

Secret map!

Create your own secret map.

First, mark the route between two chosen places with a dotted line of any shape. Mark places along the route but keep it a secret by giving each place a cryptic name and icon that only you can understand.

TRIANGLE
mountain

HOME
'x' marks
the spot!

FLYING SAUCER
(out of this world)
pizza restaurant

LOLLY
the beach

CROCODILE RIVER
busy/dangerous road

THE GIANT'S TREE
tallest building

Stain the paper with cold tea or coffee and let it dry. Then rip the edges. This will make the paper look really old! Do the same with your clues on page 55 as well.

DAILY DARE

Get up super early for sunrise.
Try and take a couple of photos.
Remember: do not look directly at the sun!

I got up at: ....

We watched it from: ....

Sunrise was at: ....

.... watched sunrise with me.

Eye spy

Spot these holiday sights.

AEROPLANE

TICKET

ADMITS ONE

MUSICIAN

UMBRELLA
(beach or rain)

FLOWERS

SUNSHINE

ART

Hello-Goodbye

You might meet people from different places on your trip. Say 'hello' and 'goodbye' in their language.

HELLO

SALUT French	**AHLAN** Arabic
BUENOS DÍAS Spanish	**NAMASTE** Hindi
CIAO Italian	**NǏ HǍO** Mandarin
HALLO German	**HALLO** Dutch
KON'NICHIWA Japanese	**GEIA** Greek

GOODBYE

AU REVOIR French	**MA' AS-SALAAMA** Arabic
ADIÓS Spanish	**ALAVIDA** Hindi
CIAO Italian	**ZÀIJIÀN** Mandarin
AUF WIEDERSEHEN German	**TOT ZIENS** Dutch
SAYONARA Japanese	**ANTÍO** Greek

Magic clouds

Watch the clouds gently roll by.

To add a challenge, see if you can find
an animal, vegetable and mineral.

SHEEP
(animal)

DAISY
(vegetable)

PARASOL
(mineral)

5 star

Write a review on any of the following:
book/today's breakfast/an activity.

What's your favourite colour?

Design a temporary tattoo!

The little things

Photograph tiny things.
It's amazing what you can miss!

TINY TOYS

DROPLETS

CRYSTALS

COOL DETAILS

PIECE OF COLOUR

LITTLE PLANTS

TEXTURE
AND PATTERN

UNUSUAL DETAILS

TEENY
CRITTERS

34

Pebble stacks

Spot these stone stacks on a track, hillside or beach anywhere in the world. Build your own or add to them with these tips.

TAKE YOUR TIME
Feel the weight of the rocks changing as you balance each stone.

A GOOD BASE
Find a flat, solid surface like a boulder or similar.

FIND GOOD SHAPES
It's easier to work with flat, smooth rounded stones.

START BIG
Start with large rocks and go smaller as you build up.

DAILY DARE

Draw it here.

Eat a food you have not tried before.

I ate: ....

It tasted like: ....

I thought it was...delicious/nice/OK/bad/disgusting!
I would/would not eat it again.

Street artist

Photograph street art you see today.
If you are out in the countryside, look out for tree
and rock carvings. In historic towns, you can often
find ancient carved graffiti too!

Try adding your
own street art!
Draw something
you saw today, then
leave it nearby for
someone to find.

Create a new ice-cream flavour!

What's your favourite thing about summer?

Traffic jam

Create an adventure holiday with words inspired by number plate letters.

MI00 PLM

For example, the letters, M, P, L, M could become Miss Paloma.

Using the number plate letters of the cars around you...

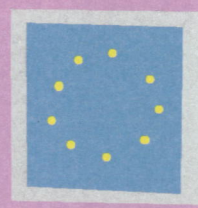 JIM 9080

...create the names of characters and places. Tell a story to your fellow passengers.

UNITED STATES OF AMERICA

9 PLK 000

 Or PLK becomes the plank on a pirate ship!

BKS 100

Take it in turns and work as a team if you like. Anyone can join in!

Take a picnic

Take a picnic with you today and find the perfect spot for eating al fresco.

SUNNY DAY

NO BALL GAMES NEARBY

NICE VIEW

SHADE

NO ANTS' NEST

BLANKET

NO WIND (SHELTER FROM WIND)

FLAT GROUND

NO ANGRY BIRDS

FAR FROM BIN

41

DAILY DARE

Try an activity that makes you nervous.

Here are some ideas!

HOLD A SPIDER

CLIMB A TREE

GO ON A ROLLER COASTER

PERFORM ON STAGE

CAREFUL
Do not take risks, stay safe.

Something special

Find or make one of these perfect holiday souvenirs for yourself or someone at home.

PRESSED PENNY

KEY RING

JEWELLERY

PAINTED STONE

SHELLS

SNOW GLOBE

Design a super-fast waterslide!

Freestyle! Draw whatever you like.

Holiday soundtrack

Listen out for unusual sounds today.
Record what you can hear on a smartphone.

Note down what you heard and where.

Local flora

Collect some tree leaves. You can use colouring pencils to create a sketch or rubbing.

SPIKY NEEDLES
Boreal forest

HUGE LEAVES
Tropical forest

FLAT LEAVES
Temperate forest

If you mostly see one type of leaf, you can tell which of the three forest types you are in.

DAILY DARE

Share something!

MUSIC
Share your
favourite songs.

MAGAZINE OR BOOK
Read aloud!

A GAME
Go two player!

ICE-CREAM SUNDAE
Just get a dessert
big enough!

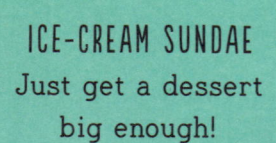

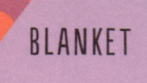
BLANKET

Journey journal

Create a diary entry about your day.

What colours can you see around you?

Invent a code for writing secret messages!

Animal detective

Go animal spotting. Did you spot these?
In a notebook, write or draw what you see.

DOG

BEETLE

BUTTERFLY

FISH

CAT

BIG
MAMMAL

52

More joy

Do a good deed today. Here are some deeds that anyone can try.

 Tell a funny joke and make someone laugh.

Put some holiday change in the charity box.

If you are away with little brothers and sisters, be nice to them! Offer to read their favourite story or just play a game they choose.

Hold the lift doors for the people coming in behind you!

Help with some tidying up. This always puts a smile on people's faces.

Smile! It's contagious.

Let's dance!

Create a dance routine or just freestyle to some music. Use these old-school moves, learn a local dance or make up your own.

ROBOT
Move like a robot. Make smooth movements with your whole body but make all your stops sharp, jerky and angular.

DISCO
This one is easy! Simply point up and then down to each spot in time with the music. Then try moving your hips in time too.

THE TWIST
Squat a bit, shake your bottom and move your arms up and down keeping your feet still.

'X' marks the spot

Create a treasure hunt for friends and family!

Here are some ideas for clues you can use. Or make up your own. Rhymes, riddles and jokes will add lots of fun to your treasure hunt!

CLUE IDEA 1:

Walk 20 strides north/east/south/west and find the

_____ to find clue number ____ .

CLUE IDEA 2:

Look up (or down/right/left) and look for the _____ .
You'll find the next clue hidden nearby in (or on/under/
behind) something shiny (or pretty/red/old/heavy/big).

CLUE IDEA 3:

Open (or shake/tickle) the_____ to find clue number __.

Make a big splash!

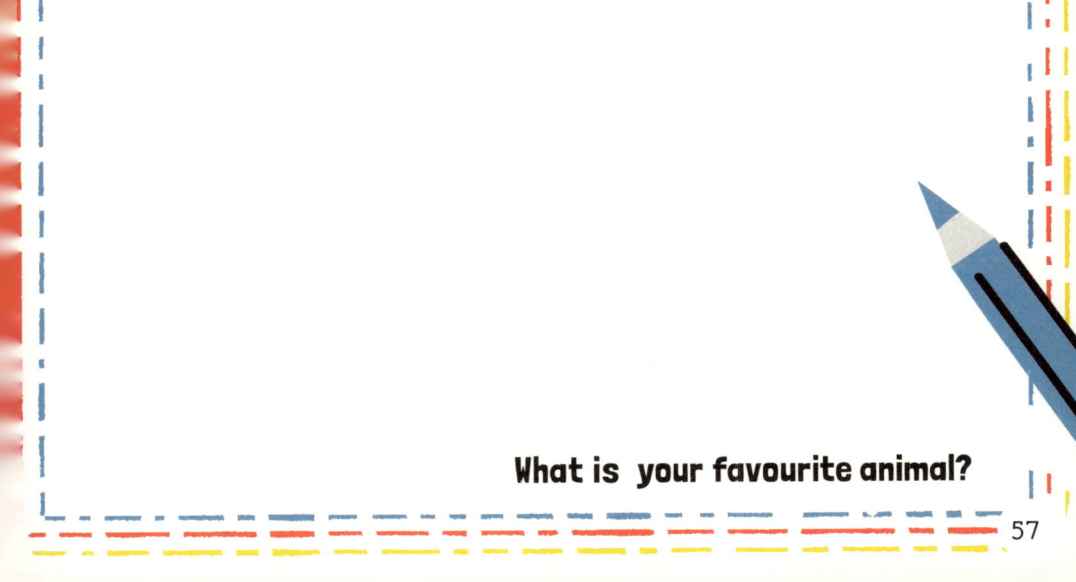

What is your favourite animal?

Holiday magnets

Decorate this fridge with souvenir magnets
from places you visited on your trip.

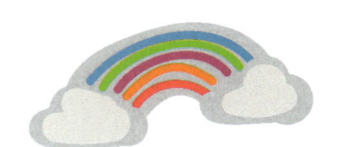

DAILY DARE

Talk to someone new!

INTRODUCE YOURSELF!

Say hello to someone your own age and maybe make a new friend...

DO YOU LIKE...?

GIVE A NICE COMPLIMENT.

...or order food, or speak to the person at the till...

PLEASE MAY WE HAVE...?

WHY IS THE...?

...or ask staff the best question you can think of.

Chef's holiday

Go to a local shop or market today and find something unusual to cook or eat with your family.

ODDITY SOUP

WACKY SAUSAGE

MAD FRUIT AND VEG

MYSTERY DESSERT

SURREAL SEAFOOD

Go online to get recipes. Or ask the seller in the shop or at the market what to do with the ingredients!

Sign it!

Collect photos of 10 unusual signs you see today. Here are some signs to get you started.

STOP!

NO DOG POO

ROAD NAME

CLOSED

WARNING SIGNS

TRAFFIC SIGNS

SHOP SIGNS

Memories

'It was all a dream...'
Oh no it wasn't! Draw or write one
memory you never <u>ever</u> want to forget.